Bear Paw Island

Wally Kasper

ISBN 978-0-9937119-3-0

Cover Photo courtesy Garry Fancy

About the Author

In 1941, Wally Kasper went straight from Leader, Saskatchewan High School to the Royal Canadian Air Force where he trained as a pilot. A year later, he was flying Lancaster bombers over Germany. He moved on to Spitfires and after the war to the University of Toronto where he studied philosophy and political science.

He was called back into the air force to teach NATO pilots and did a stint in intelligence in Europe during the Cold War. He left the air force in 1964 and went to work for CIDA setting up training programs in Canada for people round the world. He taught political science and philosophy courses at St. Patrick's, a junior college that fed universities.

He has written one book, *A night out with the boys*, on his war experiences. It had been excerpted for *Esprit de Corps* magazine. He has written many stories and poems for *Canadian Stories* magazine.

He lives in Ottawa.

Chapter One

Vancouver was a fine place to grow up, especially in the environment where I was privileged to be born. Of course, I didn't realize all this until the pleasant fabric of my life was violently torn asunder with the death of my parents in a boating accident as they were coming home from a weekend in Victoria.

Dad had been an energetic engineer who knew how to build an organization and a reputation for his engineering firm. As I was finishing high school I was gently pushed into the engineering school to follow in his footsteps.

Dad had also been an enthusiastic Scout leader so we were always very close. The forests with its wildlife of the northern regions were favorite places of mine. But somehow I could not find a great deal of enthusiasm for civil engineering. I wanted to be exploring the forest areas of northern British Columbia and paint pictures of the territory.

Dad seemed to sense this somehow and the year before I finished my engineering degree he arranged for the company to go public. The shares were snapped up and Dad arranged for a handover of the direction and he and Mom took a long overdue holiday exploring Europe.

When they were married they bought a large waterfront property, as they sold them in those days, and built a house.

When the final examinations were over we all had celebration dinner and they then told me that they were going to take four months and go through interesting places in Europe. I was delighted for them and asked if I could go to the University of Victoria and spend the summer in their fine arts studies program.

"Better than being in that big house all alone," Mom said. "After engineering it will be almost like a holiday–new places, new faces, make some new friends and enjoy yourself."

They left shortly after convocation and I bundled my things up, locked the doors and took the ferry to Victoria not knowing that this was going to be the major turning point in my life.

I drove slowly through the streets of Victoria looking at the different types of buildings. I made my way to the University buildings and found where I would be given a room and where the classes would be held. Next morning, with some difficulty I found the classroom and opened the door to make sure this was where I was supposed to be. There were about a dozen people in the room and a professor who had, apparently, just called the roll. He looked up as I opened the door, smiled and said

"Come in, come in. You are Mr. Sullivan?"

"Yes, and I'm sorry I'm late."

"No harm done, it can be a confusing place, we were just about to introduce ourselves and we have already had your name."

I looked around at four middle aged ladies sitting together, three young girls obviously just out of high school, two strangely dressed long haired types, from where I could not guess, and a young lady sitting in front of me who stood up and said, "I am Medjet, a Deerfoot, from the reserve up near Prince Rupert."

Then the professor said, "How many of you

have a university background?"

There was a moment's pause so I stood up and said, "I have an engineering degree."

Then Medjet stood up and said, "I have a law degree."

So we began and were introduced to the idea of perspective in art and then the bell rang and we were finished for the day. It was nearly lunchtime and I put my things together and wondered where there to find a cafeteria. I arrived at the elevator just as the doors were closing, and I asked another lady who was standing there if there was a cafeteria close by and she said, "One floor down."

I found something edible and fussed around over something to drink. As I left the cashier I saw an empty table off to one side. I was about to go there I heard someone say, "Would you like to join me?"

There was Medjet sitting all alone so I said, "I'd be delighted."

I put my tray down on the table and had my first real look at this young lady. She smiled and I just stared for she was the most beautiful woman I had ever seen. It took me a moment to find my tongue and then I said, "I'm Jim Sullivan, and I'm delighted to meet you. Are you a UBC grad?"

"Yes, I'm a real disappointment to my Dad, he wanted me to study engineering, but I could never wrap my head around enough mathematics to move into that world, so we compromised on my studying law. I have not done the articling yet to gain admission to the bar. I'm not sure I want to. That is why I am here. All I ever wanted to do was paint landscape pictures of the forests and regions of northern BC."

"My Dad ran an engineering firm in Vancouver but he sold it last year and now Mom and Dad are spending four months in Europe and I'm here to learn to do the painting I've always wanted to do."

Medjet and I spent a lot of time together that summer and I was determined to ask her to marry me as soon as the course was finished and my parents were back home. I had no idea what I would do for a job but there was no shortage of money in the Sullivan family after the sale of the business, so I was sure we would work something out. I was sure that Medjet loved me but we kept our relationship proper, me believing that marriage was not very far away. We spent hours in the galleries and in the library learning as much as we could about the history of art, the various schools and techniques so that when the time came for us to begin some serious painting on our own we would have an understanding of what we might do.

The course was to finish early in September. There would be a diploma for the few of us who had not fallen by the wayside. The weatherman promised a sunny day for an outside presentation of the diplomas and a reception .Mom and Dad were still four days away from the end of their holiday but Medjet said her father was going to come for the ceremony. I wasn't sure if that was good or bad for my ambition to ask Medjet to marry me but I was determined to do it at the reception..

When the graduates were presented to the public we went out to meet the various people and I caught up with Medjet and her father, a tall stern man, obviously uncomfortable in a dark blue suit and very obviously an Indian.

He noted the welcome I received from Medjet when I joined them and the way she took my hand to introduce me to her father. He stood motionless for a long moment, his eyes going from Medjet to me, and then back again. Finally, he gave me a small handshake and a nod of his head. I tried to break the ice by offering to get some drinks for us, took their orders and got into the line at the bar. When I returned with the drinks both Medjet and her father had disappeared and were nowhere to be found in the crowd. It took me a moment to understand that Medjet's display of warmth for someone with a white skin was not to be tolerated. I was almost in a state of shock with the crushing rejection. Ripping Medjet out and away was worse than a physical blow. I put the drinks down on a table and went off to the dormitory to get ready to go back to Vancouver to await the homecoming of my Mom and Dad.

Two days later came the news that Mom and Dad had been killed when two boats collided. My world became a wasteland.

Chapter Two

After tidying up the estate affairs I rented a small apartment. I found that the family home on that large waterfront lot had risen to an almost astronomical value. When the bidding war between the developers was over I found I was a very wealthy man. There was just one thing on my mind and that was Medjet. I could still feel the nasty sting of the insult her father had laid on me. In a way I could understand his pride in the ancestry, but there must be some element of compromise. I knew how Medjet felt about me. I also knew she had been trained in the law. If the tribal ties and pressures were such as to keep her from breaking free of those tribal constraints and making contact with me she would have to tell me.

She would undoubtedly have read about the boat collision in the press and would have known the casualties. Her reaction would have been to rush to be with me but obviously she had responded obediently to her father's command and cut all ties with me. His desire would be that she marry a member of the tribe and the family would continue in their ancient cultural patterns. Could these patterns be violated without breaking up her family? What did the Deerfoot community have to offer her other than a loveless marriage and an unhappy life?

I could not and would not let that happen if it was possible to rescue her from what must seem like a hopeless situation. I would channel that bright, sparkling intelligence and creative talent into avenues that would give outlet to both her world and mine. But to do anything I must go and look at that Deerfoot community, and, if possible, see her to let her know that I love her and want her to marry me. I hoped that if we could meet once more she could resist being forced into an unwanted marriage.

A government agency was very helpful in giving me accurate information as to the precise borders of the Deerfoot reserve. I could look at the region and see the limits on my movement in the area.

I bought a big new station wagon and a new set of camping equipment so I could spend the rest of the time before freeze-up examining the countryside adjacent to the western reaches of the reserve and consider my options.

The western edge of the reserve ran parallel to the main north-south highway leading up to Haynes Junction. The tribe had treaty rights of access to the ocean but did not own the waterfront property—it was still crown land and probably available for purchase.

The first of these islands was one named Bear Paw Island, a volcanic eruption in some prehistoric time. It was connected to the mainland by a small rock causeway, had some rocky projections visible from a distance and a proliferation of trees over part of its surface. I parked the car as near to the causeway as I could, put on my boots, took my rifle and went to explore the island. I went first to the rocky projection that had been thrust up and saw an astonishing formation. It was as if someone had designed three sides of a cave and then forgotten to put the roof on. From the sight and smell of the place it had been a location for hibernation of bears for a long time. The opening side faced the ocean.

As I stood in this space I was suddenly overwhelmed by the simplicity of what I was looking at. The engineering problems one would have in putting a roof on this space and turning it into an astonishing home flooded through my brain.

I went out further through the trees until I came to the other side of the island and saw that it was connected to another similar island.

I had seen no sign of wildlife as I moved through the trees and went back to the semi-cave to have another look and confirm my first impressions. The walls were solid rock; fabulous potential as thermal units which would maintain an interior temperature. It would be a simple engineering task to put a steel framework over the cave and then turn it into a large two-story house.

I went back to Vancouver and then found the government agency that controlled crown lands. There was a good deal of land in northern BC open for purchase.

They were curious about my interest in Bear Paw Island and its companion, unnamed island. They were seen as a single unit for purchase. I gave them some weak story about a fishing lodge and bought Bear Paw Island at a price they would have charged for a homesteader wanting to settle in northern BC. I got a receipt and was told it would take a few days to get the necessary papers in order. I now had to find an architect who was imaginative and could put together the plans for the structure I wanted. It took some time, the first three firms I talked to obviously thought I was nuts and told me they specialized in Vancouver residences. I did find a young Chinese architect who wasn't fully occupied and he suggested that we go up to the site and have a look.

We drove up to the island with our camping gear and found a campsite from which we could do our examination. The next day, he took elaborate note of everything and a large number of photographs, careful measurements and then he said, "You know, I doubt if there is one man in a thousand who could look at this place and see the potential you saw. There is no doubt that we can turn this place into an astonishing architectural showpiece. Lets go back home and get to work."

He took a careful look at ownership papers and then said, "Give me ten days to put together the first sketches for the roof so that the steel can be ordered."

"Ok, you proceed with your sketches. I'm going to get back to that area and go even further north on the road to Haynes Junction across the border and have a look at the countryside. I'll be back here at the end of ten days."

Getting a contractor to develop the existing causeway to the island so that trucks and heavy vehicles could cross was going to be no more complicated than building a log bridge that would support the weight. I went further up the road towards the border and after some enquiries in Haynes Junction found what I was looking for; a quarry which could produce as much really fine stone blocks for building a wing on the house to hold the car garages, workshops and a lot of storage space. It would be a bit expensive but I could buy any amount I needed and have it delivered to the island.

I went back to Vancouver for the meeting with the architect. I was surprised and delighted at what he had accomplished. Not only were the detailed sketches done, he had worked with a couple of his staff to make a small scale replica of the island and of what the house and the attached wing would look like.

"I have the steel and other materials for the roof ordered and a contractor ready to get started. If we can get the roof done while the weather is still good we can do a lot of work inside when it is bad outside."

"I have arranged with my bank to transfer a first payment of three hundred thousand dollars to your firm as soon as they have an account number for the transfer."

"The contractor will be ready to take men and material up there to build a solid permanent bridge on top of the existing causeway and an access road in to where they can set up a trailer and vehicles. Then get the cave cleaned out and the roof structure put in place. One of my apprentices has been part of the planning since we started and he will go up with the contractor's people to provide any assistance they might need."

I went back to my apartment and had a good restful sleep and then out to dinner and a movie. Home again to have a rest before I was going to go up and get close to the construction.

I didn't find out until later that the contractor had scarcely begun his bridge building before a delegation appeared and told him that he had no authority to build anything on the Deerfoot reserve and that they should stop and leave quietly. He said he was the Chief of the Deerfoot tribe.

The architect had obviously briefed his

supervisor that there might be some confusion about land ownership so the fellow assured the chief that their client owned the land, had purchased it from the BC government and that he had seen the ownership documents.

"Do you have those documents with you?" asked the Chief.

"No. Sir" he replied, "but like all land ownership documents they are available for information in the Land Titles Office."

The Chief turned to the group that had come with him and said

"Medjet, you are a lawyer, you will go to Vancouver and see who has made this land sale mistake so we can get the construction stopped."

Medjet made her way to Vancouver to the Land Titles Office and then to the Crown lands authority where they showed her the formal treaty maps with the borders of the Deerfoot reserve. She was surprised to find that the islands had been crown land indeed and the sale was legitimate and there were no grounds for dispute of the ownership.

"Can you tell me who has been the purchaser of the Bear Paw Island?" She asked.

"Of course, his name is right here–it is Mr.

James A. Sullivan."

Chapter Three

Medjet told me later that when the shock wore off she went back to her hotel and tried to call me at our old house number that, of course, had long since been "Out of service". She finally got the operator to give her a number for a J. Sullivan at a downtown address. She went through a number of Sullivans in the telephone directory. It took her a long time to find me.

I was sound asleep when the phone rang but she recognized my voice and said, "Jim, it is Medjet."

I was awake in an instant, and then said, "Where are you?"

"I'm here in Vancouver. Can we meet for breakfast tomorrow morning?"

"Yes, where and when?"

"I'm at the Empire hotel. They have a restaurant on the ground floor. Will eight o'clock be OK?"

"I'd come over right now, if I could."

"Tomorrow for breakfast will have to do. See

you then. Goodnight." The old warmth was in the voice, but obviously she had chosen a public place to meet as she was going to say a long overdue goodbye. I had a very bad night, tossing and turning but was at the restaurant at eight just as she came in. She was still the beautiful vision she had always been and seemed pleased as she smiled that radiant smile when she saw me.

I could not hold back the flood of emotions I had been feeling and as soon as the waiter disappeared I said, "Medjet, I do love you so very much. When we were at the reception before you disappeared I was going to ask you to marry me. When you disappeared that way I was devastated."

"I guessed as much and I was hoping you would but remember I am a Deerfoot with a large responsibility to my family and the tribe. My father instantly saw how we felt about each other when you were introduced and as soon as you went to get the drinks he took me by the hand and said, "We will go home where you belong."

"I saw the sad news about your parents and wanted so much to come to you but father forbad me to have any contact whatever with you. Tell me what are you doing at Bear Paw Island?"

"I'm building a home for you and me to live in."

'Father has suggested, rather forcefully that it was time I got married. He suggested a couple of men in the tribe but I have resisted each time. I do love you Jim and want very much to marry you."

She paused for a moment as our breakfast came and then went on

"Father sent me down to verify that Bear Paw Island was indeed not part of the reserve, so that the sale could be nullified. I cannot tell you how I felt when I discovered the owner was you.

"I'm going back and tell him that nothing can be changed and that since we are going to be neighbors we might as well be friends. Your appearance on the scene should wait until he cools down. We will get married, I promise you, as soon as I can manage it."

We finished our breakfasts and I asked her if she had to hurry back or did she have time to come with me on an errand up the street.

"Of course I can make the time. What do you want to do?"

"You will see when we get there –it is not far away."

So we went to a jewelry store two blocks away and went in to look for a suitable engagement ring for her. We found an eye catching splendid diamond ring and a matching wedding ring. She was delighted, but said, "I do accept and will treasure this but if I come home wearing this ring father will go into a rage which will be almost nuclear. You must keep it for me until he has accepted you and the idea of me marrying someone who is not a member of the tribe. He is the chief and very much aware of it."

She wore the ring for the rest of the morning and then took it off just before she got on board the bus to take her back to the Deerfoot village.

" I have some things to arrange in the next two days but then I will come up to Bear Paw Island to get busy with the final installations to make the place livable. The telephone is now connected so you can call me at any time."

"Any time" came sooner than either of us expected. I had two carpenters working long days to finish the interior when the phone rang. It was Medjet

"Can you help please? Father was cutting down some dead trees behind the village and a large branch fell on him and seems to have broken some bones. I am not sure what to do."

"Keep him as warm as you can, don't move him any more than is necessary. I am going to get the medevac helicopter from Prince Rupert as soon as possible. I will be right over with my emergency kit."

I found them huddled around and gave him a needle of morphine from the medical kit a few minutes before the helicopter arrived and then the para-medics took over. They strapped him down on a litter and Medjet and her mother climbed into the helicopter.

"I'll see you at the hospital this afternoon." Medjet said, and then they were gone.

I found them in the waiting room later that afternoon. A doctor came in and said, "A broken arm and a broken leg, two ribs are broken, one of which has pierced his left lung. He is sedated and will not be able to see anyone for some time. He seems to be a tough old fellow and all the signs are good. He will be here for some time so I suggest you make some arrangements for whatever he would be doing on the reserve. By the way, I think he was very lucky that you got him here as quickly as you did. It probably saved his life."

We found a comfortable room nearby for

Medjet's mother and then Medjet and I drove back to the Deerfoot village. She would get the things her mother needed and take them in next day. I went back to work on the house.

I couldn't have been more pleased with what had developed there. The roof was in place and looked like it would last a century. They had found a contractor who knew how to handle stone. He had taken a diamond surfaced polishing machine to the entire wall surface of the interior until they were as smooth as glass. When they washed the dust off of the walls the natural beauty of the stone, it's color variations and lines were magnificent.

When they were finished and getting ready to leave, the boss of the crew, a handsome Italian of the old school came to me and said, "I have traveled in many countries but I have never seen a place of such beauty. Look at the glorious reflections of the light on the walls and the floor."

"I thank you and your men for the magnificent work you have done. We will need you again in the months to come, and then you can come to see the finished product."

"Perhaps we can go fishing some time. It should be good out there."

The heavy timbers, supporting the second floor, were a thing of beauty. I wanted to be sure to get Medjet's reaction to the place when she first saw it.

A week later we had all the kitchen and plumbing facilities installed and we could now begin to live in the place in comfort. The carpenters and I were having a cup of early morning coffee when the phone rang. It was Medjet.

"I would like you to come with me to the hospital today. Can you come and can you drive? If so, can you pick me up along with some of the things I have for mother ?"

"Of course, how about me being at your place in half an hour?"

She seemed to be surprisingly happy as we drove along, and then, after a long silence she said, "Jim, I think today is going to be a very important day in our lives."

She had a grin on her face the size of the Cheshire Cat and I wondered what was behind that. We arrived in town and picked up her mother and went off to the hospital just in time for visiting hours. Her father was propped up in bed with one arm and one leg all bandaged up and greeted us as we came in. I stood back while they made a few comments and then Medjet said, " Father this is Jim Sullivan."

"I remember you from the reception at the University. I want, first of all, to thank you for what you did in saving my life after the accident. I want next to apologize for my very rude behavior at the reception. I could see that you and Medjet were attracted to each other. Like the Deerfoot I was, I wanted her to marry within the tribe. My behavior was unforgivable but you took me by surprise and all I could do was leave. I did not want to make a scene. I do apologize. Finally I understand that it is you building the house on Bear Paw Island and that you have not forgotten Medjet and she has not forgotten you. If you still want to marry her then I will give my permission and my blessings to you both and suggest that you take her home as your wife when you leave here. Again my thanks and my hearty welcome to the family."

I was speechless for a moment and then all I could say was, "Thank you, thank you."

Then I felt Medjet take my hand and she said, "I will be a good wife and we will always be close by the village." She turned to her father. "I will not cease to be a Deerfoot and I do want you to be proud of me as your child and a member of the tribe. Thank you father, we will go now and begin our new life together."

She leaned over and kissed him, I shook his hand and we left the room and went out to the waiting room. Medjet stopped for a moment, wiped some tears from her eyes and said, "My husband–I have waited so long for this day. I want so much to go to see my new home."

There was lots of afternoon light coming in the western windows and reflecting off the stone walls when she entered the large room for the first time. She stopped, seemed breathless for a moment and then said, "Oh Jim, I have never seen a room as beautiful as this."

Then she went to the windows facing the water and just looked at the ocean and the farther islands.

"How wonderful to live in a place like this."

She turned and saw the two carpenters for the first time. They had been silent as we came in so I introduced them to Mrs.Sullivan.. She smiled at them and said, "You have been doing the most wonderful things with wood in here. Has he been a slave driver?"

They laughed and one of them said, "All slaves should be as well treated and paid as we have been. We will be very sorry when the job is finished. I'm sure you will be very happy here."

It was now nearly five o'clock so I said, "Why don't you two take a few days off while Mrs. Sullivan gets acquainted with her new home"

"Thank you" one said as they gathered their tools. "The children will be going back to school in a week so our wives will welcome all the help we can give them."

They put away their tools and I went to the bedroom to get Medjet"s rings while she looked out of the windows at the magnificent view. As I came down the stairs they said their good evenings and then Medjet and I were alone.

I put the rings on her finger and she was hard pressed to hold back the tears of happiness. I held her close to me for a long time and then to break the spell I said, "Can we celebrate the day with a special dinner for your first day in your new home?"

I had planned this moment a long time ago. The shrimp with horseradish sauce followed by a fillet mignon and my favorite small potatoes that had their centers removed. The centers were mixed with a fine blue cheese and then reheated. There was a small slice of the cheese on the finished steak, together with a few pieces of white asparagus. I had a bottle of fine red wine to accompany the dinner. Medjet was wide eyed with wonder as this all appeared and after it all disappeared she helped me clear the dishes and then I served the ice cream and fresh strawberries. She ate every bite and then said, "I feel like a fairy princess whose godmother has waved a wand and made a dream come true, but I never had a dream as wonderful as my first dinner as Mrs James Sullivan. Will all of this still be here tomorrow or will it all vanish at midnight?"

"You and I and all of this and more will all be here tomorrow and our lives will begin to be full of the joy of being together and helping others in the village."

Chapter Four

After we had finished breakfast Medjet wanted to look at the ocean side of the place so we sat out on the patio and listened to the waves lapping up against the front of the steps.

The sheltered bay, the far islands, the cotton-wool clouds in a very blue, clear sky were a scene of peace and beauty.

"I would certainly like to paint this picture sometime." Medjet said.

I laughed and took her by the hand and up the stairs to the large second floor room. The door was closed but she paused and looked a second time to make sure she was reading the sign right. I had made an elaborate sign reading, "Medjet's Studio." She slowly opened the door and entered the room. Most of the wall was a series of windows so the room was alive with daylight. Then she saw the easel and all the brushes and tubes of many colors of paint and all the things painters use, laid out and ready for her. In one corner stood a desk, a filing cabinet, a telephone and a computer ready for the occupant.

She stood there speechless for a long moment and then said, "This is a dream come true, you will never know how much I have wanted something like this. It is a magical place with so much beauty."

Her delight was obvious and we went back downstairs to the small room I had taken for my office and I said, "We must give some thought to the needs that your father will have when he comes home. I expect there will be a long period of rehabilitation, time in a wheel chair and so on. There is another matter I am interested in and it is a bit delicate. I have looked around the village with some care and some of the houses are rather sadly rundown and old. They must be cold and expensive to heat in winter. Much of the village looks like it should be rejuvenated,"

"Yes," she said, "you are right. Some of them should be torn down and new ones built, but money is always in very short supply on the reserve and jobs are few and scarce. No one really knows what to do."

"Your father has been elected Chief and can

you tell me what king of authority he can exercise on the reserve?"

"He has a council of a few advisers but they seldom meet and are not much help. Without resources and money we are virtual prisoners of the system. Some, of the tribe, have gone to the cities in search of better homes and living and it has grieved father greatly to lose them, but, of course, you cannot blame them. But as to your question about authority father has given me a power-of-attorney to act in his absence."

"I have an idea that I would like to discuss with the architect and you. Can we take a couple of days off to go to Vancouver and get some basic information?"

"Of course we can"

I picked up the phone hoping Our man would be in. He was and seemed surprised to hear from me.

"All is well?" he asked.

"Indeed, but I have another matter I would like to discuss with you. Can my wife and I get some time on Thursday or Friday of this week?"

"I will be happy to keep Friday morning open for you. See you both then."

"In the meantime can we get your clothes, et

cetera moved over her so you can truly become the lady of the house?"

"If you don't need me to help you I'm going to catch a fish for lunch."

"I don't have many clothes and just a few books so it wont take long to get them here and get settled in."

I gave her a set of keys to the house and the car and in a few minutes she was gone to the village. Back an hour later she didn't have many things to bring to her new life. I promised myself that we would change that–a woman as beautiful as Medjet deserved lots of nice things and we would remedy some of that when we got to Vancouver. Our first stop next morning was the bank where she was given an account of her own and her first credit card. Then we went to Holt Renfrew and found her some fitting clothes. She was shocked at the bill but I said, "Never mind, you look beautiful."

Next morning we made our way to the architect's office, were welcomed with coffee and some cookies and he said, "What is on your mind?"

"Two things. First I want too make sure that all our bills for your services are paid, Then I want to tell you how very pleased we are with the miracle you have achieved in our home. I would also like to give you a cheque for a five hundred dollar bonus for each of those clever hard working finishing men you had working there. And then I would like to know if you know anything about crushed earth construction techniques?"

He looked at me in surprise, then stood up and went to a bookshelf, pulled out a thick leather bound book and handed it to me.

I read the inscription, University of British Columbia, Doctoral Thesis, A.Y. Chan, The history and techniques of Crushed Earth Construction. I handed the book back to him and said, "That probably answers my question."

He laughed and said, "I worked with a company which has built three houses in the islands."

"Some of the houses in Deerfoot village have seen better days. Could you give me a ball park price for a three bedroom house built in that area?"

"I would have to have a look at a number of factors before I could do that."

"Is it possible to do a comparison in cost per square foot with a wooden house, or a stone house?"

"There are so many factors of any given

location that vary widely, any figure would be just a wild guess. If you want I could send a couple of my men up there to have a detailed look and then give you a sensible answer."

"OK, please do that. But it is now getting late in the year and I assume that spring would be optimum building time?"

"Yes, but a lot of preliminary work could be done between now and then to expedite the building as soon as the better weather comes in April."

"Can I give you fifty thousand dollars to set the wheels in motion and after that can we invite you out to have some lunch?"

"I would be delighted but in about three minutes I will have a hungry wife waiting for me in the outer office."

"Can she come with us? We would be delighted to meet her."

He went to the door and moment later a beautiful, petite Chinese lady came in. We were introduced and asked them if they had a favorite restaurant we could all go to.

"One block away, with a splendid menu," his wife replied.

The two ladies seemed to find a lot of things in

common and soon became fast friends. As we said our goodbyes I was surprised to hear Medjet say, "Please come up and spend a week-end with us. The men can go fishing and we can just relax and enjoy ourselves."

Then it was back to the hotel to get out things and off to home and get organized for what might be needed when her father was released from the hospital for a long period of rehabilitation.

"What is crushed earth construction?" Medjet asked as we left the city and were out on the main highway.

"One of the oldest and long-lived methods of building. There are buildings made this way in profusion in Australia in recent years and many in other countries which are centuries old and still in use. They get a proper mixture of soils and churn the soils up after they are poured into a framework. The process is labor intensive and takes up to a hundred days to take its final consistency. It can be shaped any way you like in the framework and when finished is as hard as concrete and very nearly indestructible."

"Just a proper mixture of soil as it base?"

"Yes."

"And Alan, our architect friend, knows how to do this?"

"Yes, he apparently has built a few of them, or at least worked for a company over on the island which has built three such houses on the islands."

"And you are thinking of introducing this process to the Deerfoot reserve?"

"Building a house like this for your parents could serve as a guide to creating a beautiful village. With that forest available there is a great deal of potential there. Do the Deerfoot tribe have a long history of totem poles?"

"Yes they have but they have been badly neglected in the past forty years. I would like to see the practice renewed. Totems seem to add so much character to a village. Father has an album of pictures of some early days and they were very imaginative and colorful."

She was quiet and thoughtful until we arrived home. It was now dark and as I turned on the lights as we came in she was spellbound at the reflections coming off of the walls.

"You must be starving. Would you like chicken, fish or beef for your dinner?"

"We had that splendid beef last night. Can I

learn how you do a chicken dinner? Can I help?"

"Of course. The chicken is fried without oil, the sweet potato fries likewise, and the onion rings come with a special batter on them, nice and crisp."

We made our way through a few smoked salmon tidbits and a glass of wine until the timer rang and then we feasted on the chicken. A chilled sliced pear and then we sat in front of the fireplace with our coffee. She looked at the fire for a while and then said, "I must truly have died and gone to heaven."

We cleared away the dinner dishes, tidied the kitchen and then went back to the chairs in front of the fireplace. I turned on a Beethoven symphony and we each found a book to read.

Suddenly she sat up and said, "This room needs a big brown bear rug here in front of the fireplace. And I know where the rug is."

She picked up the phone, and after a moment said, "George, this is Medjet, do you still have that large brown bear rug?"

"I have two of them, the large one from last year and another that was caught earlier this year. It is the largest one I have ever seen and the fur is perfect."

"I want to buy it, what is the price?"

Medjet, we owe you a lot and since you are a member of the tribe I'll give you a special price."
I can deliver it tomorrow if you wish."

"That would be perfect." and then she said to me, "This will be a one in a lifetime chance for something like this and you and the house deserve it. It is so extravagant that I feel guilty."

"Medjet, I should tell you that the house that I grew up in in Vancouver was on a large waterfront property that my Mom and Dad had purchased some forty five years ago for ten thousand dollars when they were first married. When the estate was settled and the property went up for sale there was a bidding war between some developers and the place was finally purchased for five million dollars. Erase the guilt feelings from your mind and give your friend a fair price as we are going to have to live with him for a long time."

When the bearskin rug arrived next morning and we laid it out in the reading room in front of the fireplace I was amazed. It was certainly the largest I had ever seen, the fur was perfect and this fellow must have been an old male dominating the bears in the region. I hoped that he had left his genes abundantly before he went to his end. The rug was so impressive that I knew what he was asking was a markdown for Medjet and was not a fair price. I told him so and made the cheque out for an extra four thousand dollars. He was pleased and we certainly had a bargain.

She was sipping a cup of coffee when the fellow left and after a while said, "Will you take me out in the boat some distance out in the bay this afternoon? I would like to do some sketches of the house and the island and then do a large oil paining to go on that wall, a perfect setting for such a picture."

Chapter Five

Our next trip to the hospital had a curious result. While we were sitting in the waiting room a couple came in with an adorable white poodle on a leash. They sat down beside us and after a few minutes of silence the dog made a small noise underneath the chair of its owner. Some other people looked up and the owner said to her husband, "Damn dog is just a nuisance. I wish we had never gotten him from the kennel"

Medjet looked at the lady, and saw that she was quite serious so she said, "I would be very happy to buy the little fellow if you are serious."

"We paid one hundred dollars for him three weeks ago. He is a pure bred and we have the pedigree papers. If you will give us fifty dollars for him you may have him right now and we will send you the papers for him."

Medjet produced the money and gave them our address. Then turning to me she said, "I know this was hasty but he is such an adorable little fellow. I have wanted one like him since I was a child"

She took him up and held him in her lap as she scratched his ears and then took him out to the car so we could go in and see her father. As we left she drove and went right to a pet supply shop to buy a bed and all the things we would need for him.

It took him a couple of days to accept his new people and environment and then he became a happy well-loved member of the family.

We took him with us on a walk into the trees around the island and, of course, he found an endless supply of new smells and curious things to explore. He ended up by marking these things with his scent. I watched this for a while and then said to Medjet, "He seems to take a great delight in shooting at so many objects–I suggest we call him Gunner."

Medjet laughed and said, "It would be fitting indeed."

It was surprising to see how he bonded with Medjet and seemed to follow her around. Two weeks later he began to earn his keep.

We never thought a great deal about security because we assumed our remote location was enough protection from intruders. One evening we were watching a TV movie and went to bed late and as usual left the door to the outer shed unlocked. Now Gunner's bed was just inside the door as one came into the house from the attached shed. An hour later we were awakened by loud barking from Gunner, then heard the door of the shed slam shut and looking out of the window saw two shadowy figures running in the direction of the causeway and the main road. Gunner got his ears scratched, we locked the door and all went back to sleep.

We had spent many hours clearing some of the undergrowth and deadwood on the island, it added to the beauty of the forest as well as giving us lots of wood for the fireplace. Then I cut down many of the birches as they seemed not to thrive on the soil on the island. The conifers seemed to be a variant of the Colorado blue family and were magnificent.

I wondered if any of the bears who had hibernated in the old cave would remember and be back when the cold weather arrived. If they came around Gunner would certainly let us know.

One Friday morning early in October Medjet and I were sitting out on the patio drinking coffee and watching the waves break against the dock. A splendid large cabin cruiser came slowly into the bay and then took a place against the dock. Christine, the architect's wife, jumped onto the dock, tied the boat up to the pylons and gave us a hearty "Good morning" Alan, her husband, shut off the engines and they joined us on the patio.

"Welcome to Bear Paw Island. Would you like to come in and have some breakfast?"

"We were awake early and had some breakfast but coffee would be most welcome."

Over coffee Alan said, "One of my clients took a beating in the stock market and offered the boat to cover a payment on a property he was developing. It is nearly new and has been superbly designed by a Vancouver builder so we took it on and thought we would surprise you by an impromptu visit. Nice to get out to do some fishing as well as a bit of business."

Christine had been looking at the polished stone walls reflecting the sunlight. Then she saw the large picture of the house and island that Medjet had completed and she went over for a better look. After a moment she said, "Oh Alan, I want one of these for our living room." Then to Medjet she said, "What gallery did you get this from and who is the artist of this marvelous painting?"

Medjet laughed and said, "Thank you for the compliment. I did the painting and have yet to put my signature on it. I have four others underway in my studio upstairs. You may choose one for later delivery. I'm experimenting with some shades of color and you are my first critique of the technique. I'm pleased and flattered by your reaction to the picture. Would you like to come up and choose one of the scenes I have begun?"

Over coffee Alan said, "I have a classmate friend from architectural school days who is now a senior director in the federal Government Indian affairs Ministry. Over lunch he told me about a not well-known government program to assist tribes in upgrading the villages on the various reserves. They will provide grants under certain conditions for rebuilding residences and other buildings to up-grade the village. The direction you have suggested was new to them. He was intrigued by the prospects and would welcome an opportunity for detailed discussions which he might take to his Minister."

I looked at Medjet and saw that she was as excited about the potential as I was. Alan went on to say, "How many Deerfoot families are there in the immediate vicinity and can you guess at the number farther away from the reserve?"

Medjet says, " There are about thirty families in and close by the village and about the same number scattered in the city areas."

Alan said his estimator team has developed a rough plan based on available water supply and other resources that would make crushed earth construction possible and very workable in this area. If the tribe could produce two million dollars the government would pay for infrastructure development and match the money for building permanent houses and other buildings. The start-up program will produce about twenty three bedroom houses and a large assembly long house.

Medjet said, "Two million dollars? The tribe does not have that kind of money."

I said, "This would be a long term investment and I'm sure we could raise that much money for this purpose. It is now October so I assume you could make necessary procurement arrangements before spring brings good weather. We can start building at that time. "How many of these houses could you build in one year?"

"Ten or twelve."

"We could hold a meeting of the tribe and hold

a lottery, once the first families were in place we could get the next phase underway. Medjet has power of attorney as acting chief but we will discuss this in detail with her father and get his approval. I think that will be a formality, and you may feel confident as of this moment with Medjet's approval. Tell me how much money should be transferred to you for the initial activity. Now, how about some lunch and then we can go fishing. I want to teach Medjet how to talk down the line to the big fish so they take the bait."

"Yes, yes, can you teach me the words to use?" asked Christine.

"I must warn you that there are dangers involved. Last week we had a fish that was so large, that when we finally got him near the boat it was obvious, that he would swamp the boat if we brought him on board so we had no choice but to cut the line and let him go."

Medjet had looked surprised as I told the fish story to Alan and Christine and when I was finished she said, "Yes, yes, and if you believe that fish story I have some old mining stock which you will be most anxious to buy."

Then to Jim "Jim would you like to get a nice

salmon poaching on the barbecue for lunch? I'll take our guests up to the studio and show them my partially finished paintings."

Gunner and I stoked up the barbeque and wrapped a salmon after a generous dose of tarragon and white wine and then contemplated the cooking of some white asparagus to accompany the salmon.

When we had finished lunch and were dawdling over coffee we were surprised to hear the doorbell ring. Gunner was in good voice and we were delighted to see the very clever Italian stone and marble wizard who had done the cutting and polishing in the house. They had been very precise in getting the walls straight, the corners perfect. We had noted that he had been very careful to collect the salvage that we thought was throw away material. He had heard Medjet and I talking about chess one day and noted it in his memory. When they were all finished with their work in the house everything was neat and tidy. Medjet and I could not have been more pleased. The next time we were in the city we stopped by to tell him so and gave him a well deserved bonus for the men who had done a difficult job so well. Things had been quiet in his shop and he had cut, from the salvage stone, a number of pieces to make a chessboard. The board was supported by a pedestal cut from square pieces of stone. It could only be described as a work of art. They had come on this quiet Saturday to see if they could look at the finished house and give us the table with their thanks and best wishes. They wanted to take some photographs, so we produced a couple bottles of red wine, a cheese board and some crackers and had a nice visit with these clever Italian workmen.

Curious how these things interweave in our lives, but it happened, that Christine's grandmother had passed away two months ago and they needed someone who could produce a headstone for the grave in the Chinese fashion. Christine asked the workmen if it was possible to submit some sketches for discussions. They said, "No problem".

When they left, we thanked them, Christine made arrangements to meet to confirm the headstone design and then Alan said, " I know who will be doing the floors of our house building program next spring". Turning to Medjet he said, "Could they be given traditional Deerfoot symbols to look at and suggest how they might be incorporated in the floors of a house?"

Medjet smiled and said, "We have built a file

of traditional designs as they have appeared in totem poles and other native art forms. I will give them copies to study."

Alan said, "Of course totem poles, I had forgotten completely about them. We must have a few and get someone started making them as soon as possible. What wood will live long and be suitable for the kind of carving that must be done? Do you have a local expert who can be asked to work on this project? If there is one thing that will really impress the first stage of building this village, it will be some colorful totem poles.

I'm all excited, thinking of what the Italians can do, when we build the first longhouse for the community assembly hall out of the stone that we can get at a most reasonable price from the quarry near Haynes Junction. They want to keep the place going and not lose their skilled hands, so we will get a marvelous product at a knock-down price."

After a long lazy dinner the first day we went and sat in front of the fire in the reading room and Christine saw the great bear rug for the first time.

"Oh Alan, I want one for our recreation room."

He looked at her in dismay and said, "I'm not sure which end of a rifle produces a bullet and I don't think these things grow on trees."

Medjet laughed and said, "Believe it or not, we have been known to have some of them in our back yard. Some of the older ones have become quite dangerous and must be culled out for public safety. But this process is carefully supervised. Heavy fines are levied on hunters who shoot the young females who are minding their own business in the back forests."

She picked up the phone, dialed a number, and then said, "George, it is Medjet. Do you still have that bearskin rug available? You do? Good. We have some visiting friends who would like to look at it. Could you come over after breakfast tomorrow?"

Then to Christine, "It is a beautiful bearskin, not as large as this one. The bear was killed by George up near Haynes Junction where it had been doing damage to the garbage dump and terrorizing the school."

Later, Medjet noted Christine's reaction as George unrolled the rug and then nodded to George who understood that he had made a sale, thanked Medjet and left.

A few moments later Christine noticed that George had left and said, "He is gone. What do we do now?"

"You take the rug home with you and when we finish your painting we will tidy up the details." Then to Alan, "Each of the totem poles will have to serve a long time and be capable of being repainted every five or seven years. Boat builders know a lot about protective varnishes these days and a cracking good job on the totem poles will help a great deal in catching the attention of the public. We must find a really good hard wood and get started as soon as possible. We can get a steel workshop set up and get a couple of the good carving men to work. The shop must be long enough to have the log laid out and then space for them to have the paint dry properly before the varnish goes on."

Alan and Christine left the next day to get back from their first cruise and go to work. It was going to be a very busy fall and winter season both at the architects' office and the Deerfoot village.

Chapter Six

Before Alan and Christine left that morning it occurred to me that there were few organizations in the province that knew more about quality and longevity of wooden poles than BC Hydro. Alan smiled and said, "Of course, I should have guessed that. I'll be on to their experts tomorrow and see what we can find out about the best wood and its availability."

A week later two trucks pulled up to the village and then the crew began to assemble a long steel shed and an array of cutting and grinding tools.

Two days later another truck appeared and offloaded a dozen long wooden poles, which we quickly put on stands in the shed so they could dry out and the work could begin.

Medjet had found two of the tribe who had some knowledge and experience with totem poles. They spent hours with Medjet on the designs and were anxious to get started.

We held a meeting of the tribe in the old hall and I proposed, that the tribe could get into some economic activities, which would produce revenue for the building program. For example we could take a hundred acres of the dense forest, mostly birch and conifers and set it aside as the future ranch area for beef cattle production. First we needed a team of men who would go over the area and clear off the birch and the undergrowth. This could be cut and stored and sold in the city as premium firewood. When the ranching area had only the conifers left there would be a stand of the original buffalo grass. It was good grazing for cattle and we could easily obtain and spread a couple of tons of potash and scatter a lot of clover to improve the nutritional quality of the grazing. As the land was cleared, we could get the fencing in to keep the predator animals out and then begin the development of a high quality beef herd. There was a meat packing plant in Prince Rupert so a constant market was assured.

One day late in October, just before the first snow arrived, Medjet, Gunner and I were out having a walk around the island. As we got to the other side where there was a drop off of some feet to the water's edge I noticed, again, a curious increase in the speed of the wind. Farther out across the water there were two unoccupied islands that formed a kind of V shape and it seemed, that the wind was almost constantly blowing in this natural channel. I knew that farmers on the prairies had, for many years, been using windmills with electricity producing accumulators and a battery hook-up system. With this wind flow being almost constant, why would we not install a series of these smaller windmills and produce all the power we needed in the village. The main BC Hydro line was only a short distance away and maybe we could sell our excess production to BC Hydro. Power production plants were a long distance away so delivery charges were high up here. Maybe a reasonable investment could save the tribe a lot of money over the years.

I raised the matter with Alan a few days later and he laughed and said, "It looks like God has given you a licence to print money. It is so simple that you wonder it hasn't been done before. Can I bring a couple of my experts up there to have a look and do some measurements tomorrow? Certainly, all the technology is available and Hydro would pay premium prices for all the electricity you can put into the grid."

We all went out to the site the next day and Alan stood in the sharp wind flow and said, "All it took was a stroke of genius to recognize the potential. We can easily put up a steel frame to hold five or seven windmills. I assume that the wind-flow may vary slightly from daytime to night but that doesn't matter. Let's see how fast we can get the structure up and the windmills turning?"

"Do you think you can get it all together and in place before it is too cold for outside work?"

"We can give it our best shot. You haven't noticed any bears returning to the island to hibernate, have you?"

"No, Gunner seems to be on duty twenty four hours a day and would let us know."

We had lunch and when they were ready to leave Medjet gave Alan two large rolled up items in protective covers and said, "One is the picture Christine wanted and the other is the picture you liked. I thought it might be nice in your office. Transporting them on their frames from here to Vancouver is difficult so perhaps you and Christine could find suitable frames and have them mounted."

"Christine will be so pleased, and I don't know

how to thank you."

The weather continued to be typical late fall and the forecast was favorable. They moved the crew up to the island, leveled the terrain for the framework and had the towers in place in three days. Then the supporting framework to hold the windmills went in place and by the end of the ten days they had the windmills mounted and working. They were meticulous in checking the functioning of every item in the system. When they finished, hey told us that the hydro inspectors would be coming along the next day to check the installation and put the metering system in place.

While I had been watching the electrical production process Medjet had been keeping a close watch on the totem pole production. She had laid out the original sketches in bright eye-catching colors, after all they were going to be an integral part of showcasing the new village and she wanted them to be perfect. It was a lot of work to seal and then prime the wood before the first coat of paint went on, but when the colors were put on according to the sketches the whole thing seemed almost to come alive. The final coats of varnish would protect the colors for years to come.

Medjet's father and mother had come back to the village after a long period of rehabilitation and were most pleasantly surprised at the changes that had been made. They had a careful look at the first finished totem pole and then her father suggested that the whole tribe should be brought together for a meeting and a dinner to celebrate the beginning of the new village. He wanted to rebuild the ancient pride that the Deerfoot people had taken in their culture and their place. He wanted to bring forward for public recognition the men who had done so very much work in clearing the rangeland and the ones who had done the splendid work on the totem pole. The tribe was going to rebuild the Deerfoot way of life.

One of the men who had been doing the range clearing reported to the assembly that after the underbrush was cleared and the grazing was easier there were a large number of deer that found their way into the rangeland. There was a small stream of clear water running through the rangeland so the living was easy for them.

Medjet stood up and asked why the tribe could not raise a herd of deer as well as a herd of cattle. There were enough people who remembered the way the deerskins were tanned and then made into Deerfoot jackets for the adult members of the tribe. They were very functional and distinctive and could be a source of pride for the members.

Medjet had, with help from Christine, incorporated the village under provincial law. In the village there were a number of committees, each with a given function and responsibility. This made it easy to assign human resources and maintain financial control of all the activities in the village.

A group of four women knew how the traditional tanning process of deerskin had been done. As soon as the hunters brought in a few deer skins they went into action producing the finest buckskin leather to hand over to the committee which was going to tailor the men's and women's jackets.

The Chief called an assembly meeting and dinner and then proudly presented the first sets of husband and wife jackets to the applause of all the members.

The hunting member brought in a half dozen of the old bucks from some of the herds. They did the butchering of the animals and shared the venison with the village families so each family had a good supply in their freezers. When the rangeland, we had planned, was cleared and re-planted it became obvious that we had underestimated the need for land. We finished the fencing and awaited the arrival of the deer. It didn't take long for them to come into the rangeland. Then we put the first of the Black Angus beef herd in to see if the deer and the cattle could live together.

The village was a very busy place over the winter. They were busy restructuring the ancient patterns of the Deerfoot culture.

They understood once more that they were without question given a fair share of the venison. When the fish run arrived, they were given a fair share of fish. All were members with equal status in the community and knew that they must pull their weight in the tribal family. They were happy, well cared for and proud to be Deerfoot.

The winter snow vanished early and the hunters were busy, the ladies were working at top speed and everyone was happy.

Suddenly it was spring and Alan's first crews arrived to begin the preparation for building the first of the crushed earth houses for the village. Medjet's father and mother moved in with us as their house was at the entry to the village and the first to be replaced. None of the houses would have a basement as the topsoil was not very thick on top of the solid rock formation.

Alan came to the first construction to test the soil mixture and make sure the formula was right. The frames were laid in place and the Deerfoot adventure had begun.

Three and a half months later the first house exterior was completed and our Italian stone workers moved in to do the floor. They had worked closely with Medjet on the Deerfoot symbols that were to be inlaid. They were eye-catching as one entered the front door and would last for centuries and would be easy to clean for the housekeeper. The kitchen people had designed a kitchen based on what we had in our house. Any woman would be pleased to have such a layout.

Medjet's mother had been very close to her daughter in the time they spent with us so there was nothing new there.

The stonemasons had put a large stone support slab in front and to one side of the house and put in place the stone holder for the totem pole. When it was all in place we took the Chief and his lady to their new home and invited the other families to come and share the celebration.

There were seven other houses in various stages of building. We had arranged a lottery at an earlier assembly to draw names to see who would get a house in the first building phase.

Alan had proved to be a master at controlling each part of the building process. When the exterior of the house was finished the Italian stone masters were ready to do the floors, each a different design, and then the kitchens went in and the house was ready for occupation.

It was a busy summer in the village, to say the least. When the seventh house was completed and the totem poles were all in place the Chief sent a formal note to the Minister. He invited him and his staff to come to look at what had been accomplished in the first phase of rebuilding the village and the community.

To our surprise, unforeseen things began to happen. When the expanded rangeland was cleared and the random clover planted, the grazing for the cattle seemed to be ideal. It had also been noticed by several small groups of deer. When we took the first group of beef cattle to the meat packing plant in Prince Rupert they were most pleased and asked for more. We asked them if they were interested in venison. We were told that they had no knowledge of what sort of market there was but they were prepared to take some three-year old deer and see how the market responded. Three months later we had our answer. The retailers were astonished at the sales and requested more.

We got the rangeland clearing committee back in action and expanded the grazing area by another hundred and sixty acres, did the fencing and became deer ranchers on a much larger scale.

There was a nice spin off as we made a surprising amount of money selling the tanned deer hides. The ladies carefully chose three-year old hides for making the Deerfoot jackets for the tribe members.

One of the ladies said she knew how to deal with bee keeping and since there were now large areas of clover in the rangeland why did we not get a few hives and start producing some honey for the members?

When the house building stopped for the season Alan doubled the workers at the construction site for the stone long house. He thought he could get the outer shell done and the windows installed before the bad weather came. The interior could be completed in the days and weeks to come.

This was the first venture of the Deerfoot tribe into building with stone and it became a source of pride for all. Shortly after the basics were installed in the kitchen, three magnificent trophies appeared. A huge black bear skin rug, the largest set of antlers we had ever seen and a twelve-foot fish mounted for display. These things were hung on the wall at the front and certainly caught the attention of anyone who came into the building.

The Chief could hardly have been more pleased and suggested that the tribe should have a meeting on a Friday evening. They could hear reports from the committees, hear of the planning for future building and activity, and then share in a venison chili feast. The Chief was going to do everything he could to build the people's pride in their ancient traditions and way of life. He wanted them all to get to know each other well and to share as much of their lives with each other as they could. This would build trust and dependence and help the tribe to grow. He knew that there was an unknown number of Deerfoot in the cities, some of them living wretched lives because they had abandon their ancestral habitat for what they had hoped might be better opportunity for them and their children.

Alan had hired a public relation firm to put pictures of the village in the press and magazines. This initial program was only province wide but we would see what results grew out of it.

Chapter Seven

The winter months passed quickly as everyone was busy with either finishing details of the new buildings or with the planning for next year's building.

In mid February we had another visit from Alan and Christine. The waterways were open and they had brought their planning documents for a detailed discussion.

Alan had a breakdown of the cost factors for the houses and we were surprised to see that the labour costs were as high as they were. He said, "If we could significantly reduce the cost of the workers, we could build ten or eleven houses instead of seven next season."

Detailed reports had been sent to both the federal and provincial government. Alan was surprised at how well they had been received and both had promised funding support for the next building phase.

Since the next assembly evening for the tribe was only a few days away we proposed that they stay and attend. They might be able to answer some questions from the members.

The ladies' committee had produced a masterly venison chili dinner. When everyone was finished and the place tidied up, the Chief called the meeting to order and asked for a financial report from Medjet. She surprised them all by outlining how, for the first time in decades the village had a substantial savings fund available. She poured praise on the men in the rangeland clearing committee for the money they had brought in from the firewood sales and then the committee that controlled the cattle and venison production.

She then raised the matter of labour for house building in the up-coming season.

"All of you have seen the houses which have been built so far. We need more houses for the families and we would like to get as many done this season as possible. If we could cut the labour cost to a minimum we could produce ten or eleven houses instead of seven as we did last year. All of you know where your names are on the list made up at the lottery so you know when your house will be ready for you. How many of you would offer to take a significant cut in wages and work on the houses as needed to get more of them sooner. You know the tribe would do everything they can to make meat, fish, vegetables available for you to ensure you and your families are supported as the village building goes on."

Ever man in the hall raised his hand.

Medjet smiled and then went on, "There is another matter that I have wondered about for a long time, and that is can we build a house of worship for the community, a house not devoted to any particular cult, sect or religion. It could be an ecumenical meeting place and we could establish the cemetery close by. How many members would like to see such a building and should we establish a committee to look into the matter and report back at a later meeting? Please indicate your agreement by raising your hand."

"Against? No one.

The Chief adjourned the meeting and all the people went home, Later as the four of us were sitting in the living room over some coffee Medjet said, "I wasn't sure how the suggestion for a house of worship would be accepted. There are too many horror stories around about church schools and so on. Secondly few things could be further from the Deerfoot ancestral patterns than a stone church with stained glass windows. If we started a pattern of an ecumenical speaker followed by a breakfast of pancakes for all attendees every Sunday morning we would soon expand the attendance and active participation."

Then she turned to Alan and said, "Have you built any churches lately?"

"None, I'm afraid. We seem to be a heathen lot. Let me see what I can come up with by way of design sketches."

I wondered what one would represent in a stained glass window that had no Christian religious connotation. Could we duplicate a pastoral scene like one of my landscape paintings in a window? And could several different windows, choosing colors taken out of the reserve settings be made? Could we possibly make windows of that kind for a building in the village? I guessed there must be a school that trained people in the making of stained glass windows in Vancouver. Could we get a couple of our people in there and see what they could learn? Since our large building was made of a beautiful stone, and would be there for centuries why not see if we could enhance the beauty with stained glass windows?.

I spoke about the idea to Medjet who said, "Not very traditional for the Deerfoot tribe, but then we have made virtually everything new. It should add greatly to what we have already created here. Is it affordable?"

"The two most artistic people I know in the tribe are the newly married Wagstaff couple. They are due to get the next house that we build so some months of training would make the least dislocation in their lives".

We found the school and outlined what we were looking at as a long-range program. The Director was amused at first at the idea of an Indian tribe with stained glass windows, but came around soon enough when we took him out to the building and he saw what the end product would look like.

Not only would he be pleased to supervise the training of the Wagstaff couple, but he would ensure the best possible first two windows be installed in the assembly hall. The Director of the school looked carefully at the construction of the building, realized that here was a radical departure from what had been

Indian patterns and realized that these structures were going to be here for centuries to come. He wanted to be part of the history of those years so he and the school would help in every way they could.

The first totem pole was almost complete so we would have workshop space available for use. In mid February, Alan advised us that the weather forecast was very favourable and wondered if they could get started early in the construction program. We were happy to give him a green light on an early start and called the men together to ensure available labour as the construction proceeded,

The first house frames were up in a week and the earth crushing process begun.

Then Medjet got a call from a lawyer of one of the large oil companies. They wanted to run a pipeline underground through part of the reserve territory. Could they send a team up to the village for discussions?

Of course, Medjet called Christine and asked her to come up and assist with negotiations. It might be the source of a significant amount of welcome funds to help in the village expansion program.

It was apparent from the beginning of the meeting that the company was expecting to get their pipeline approval for a paltry sum, but they had not reckoned with someone as clever and experienced as Christine. She had done her homework prior to the negotiations and discovered that the company had no real option but to put the pipeline through Deerfoot territory. They had virtually no room for negotiation. They would pay a half a million dollars as an initial payment and an annual fee based on the amount of oil they moved through the pipeline. The reserve would get a handsome annual input of welcome cash to use for the building program. The tribe would have to say a real Thank You to Christine.

Medjet had her sketches for the house of worship, and we now had to develop the setting for the house and its related cemetery. It would have to be protected from wild animals from the forest area and such fencing was going to be prohibitive in cost. Enquiries at a Vancouver nursery turned up a clever expert who had emigrated from England and he knew how to plant a thorn shrub border which would keep animals out, require little care and would be inexpensive but require a good deal of labor for the installation. It could be done in easy stages.

When the first totem pole was finished one of the clever young men who had been busy with design came to the Chief with an idea. He said there were a good number of stumps of birch and other trees in the rangeland. Usually, these were pulled out, and burned to get rid of the debris. Most of these stumps could be pulled out, cut into a basic block and then, after cleaning, drying and removing the dead roots they could be easily turned into an irregular shaped wooden bowl. With a bit of sanding and polishing, after the inside wood had been removed, one would have a beautiful irregular shaped bowl for use and decoration in the house. Could they make a half a dozen of them and see if there would be a significant response in a shop in Vancouver?

They started with six. No two were the same in shape and size. They carefully recorded the hours required to make each one. When they were done they were placed in a gift shop in Vancouver. They attached a small booklet about the Deerfoot tribe to each, decided to ask a premium price and all of them were sold in the first two days they were on display.

The men working on these wooden bowls had a visit from the Chief a few days later. He admired what they were producing and congratulated them on this scheme and then said, "I think you are going to get some noise from the ladies at the next assembly. You might want to think about that."

When the business meeting rolled around at the next assembly Medjet reported a nice amount of money had come into the tribe's account from the sale of the artisans woodworking shop. The Chief congratulated the men and then one of the ladies rose and said, "The men who have been doing the woodwork are all wearing handsome buckskin jackets that we made for them. Now we would like to have some of these wonderful bowls that they are making."

Then Jason the chief designer of the group and two of the men went to the back of the hall and brought some boxes forward, laid out a dozen bowls and said, "There is a great deal of difference from one tree stump to another. We have been saving the most distinctive and beautiful so that the ladies of the tribe could have the best. It is slow work culling out the finest ones and we have brought the first of for your examination. We would also like the ladies to make the decision as to the distribution of these bowls. We would like to continue with selecting the best for our ladies and will bring along some more for the next assembly. May I say that there is no man in the artisan's group who is not most grateful to the ladies for their superb work in making the jackets we are so proud of and we would like to say Thank You to the ladies who have made them."

The men of the tribe were busy indeed that season. When there was a slack time in the house building for a few days they were out helping the rangeland committee pulling tree stumps and leveling the holes so the deer and cattle could range freely.

South of the reserve territory, there was a large stand of trees on crown land. The government had approved some very selective cutting of red pine trees, and when we approached the authorities and asked if we might go on to this land and remove some stumps they thought we were mad but happily approved the removal of all we wanted. We rented a tractor and chains and took out a dozen stumps and took them back to the village. These were tree stumps from old trees so they were different to work with than the birch we had taken in the past. It took the design people some time to finally cut the large trimmed stump into four sections. Beautiful, hard and red in color they turned them into floor masterpieces- works of art which would surely be kept at home for use in the assembly hall..

It was obvious that there was a gold mine in the tree stumps that were there for the taking. The crown land authorities thought that this Indian tribe was mad, but they welcomed the departure of the stumps as it would make the reforestation much easier.

The next time Jason rented the tractor they pulled three large loads of stumps, trimmed them on site and took them back to the village. Trimmed and washed they were stacked ready for a winter's hard work.

On his next visit to the workshop of the artisans the Chief took Jason aside and said, "Would you consider a presentation of one of your best for Medjet and Christine? After all they have made significant contributions to the village."

Jason went to a cupboard and opened the doors so the Chief could see the bowls on the shelves.

"We have kept some of the finest here now that all the ladies have them. Choose two of them for Medjet and two for Christine and we will deliver them to Medjet's house tomorrow."

Christine and Alan arrived in their boat for a visit on the weekend. Christine could hardly have been more pleased. She phoned the Chief and Jason to say Thank You. Then, turning to Alan, said, "

You should have one of these in your office where it will be seen by many people".

Alan spent some hours with his senior staff inspecting the construction program and then came back to the house quite satisfied with the way things were progressing..

They decided that they would like to have a mini-holiday fishing, loafing around and cruising through the islands. Every one was enjoying the time , Gunner most of all.

Then our holiday was interrupted by a phone call from the Director of development of Crown Lands. The property that lay adjacent to the reserve in the south had been designated as potential farmland and should be available for assigning homesteads for immigrant new comers to the province. There was a problem though. The land had been clear-cut by a timber company that had not been able to fulfill its responsibility in clearing the land of stumps and deadwood. Since the Deerfoot people had already removed a number of stumps the government was prepared to offer them thirty dollars per stump if they would remove all of them from the territory and would pay the same fee for those already removed. Their inspectors counted seventy-three removals already done and counted another ninety three for clearing the entire property. They would like the property cleared this season, if possible.

Medjet hung up the phone and laughed out loud as she called her father and Jason inviting them to come over for a short business meeting.

After listening carefully Jason said

"There is probably ten or fifteen thousand dollars worth of good birch firewood for the taking there, and you know the value of the stumps for the woodworkers. Call the fellow back and tell him we will have a clean-up crew on the land tomorrow morning. Ask if he would like to give us permission to do the same kind of clean up on the property to the north of the reserve land."

While we were having coffee after Jason had left I said to the Chief, "There is a curious formation of two circles of maple trees at the western end of the reserve. Maple trees are unusual out here and these two circles, one inside a larger outer one, could not have occurred naturally."

"Of course, I had forgotten all about them. My grandfather planted them when he was trying to expand the activities of the tribe. They have long been forgotten."

"They should be in their prime now and should be capable of producing enough first class maple syrup to serve the needs of the tribe."

" I will enquire as to the cost of a frost fence around the cluster and as to the taps and lines for collecting the syrup in the spring. We will need a small steel shed and boiling vats and a large supply of containers for the syrup."

We cleared the underbrush around the trees, fertilized the land generously, watered the area as well as we could and then waited for the spring to arrive. As soon as the sap started to run we set the whole machine in motion and began the gathering and boiling. We tested some samples on the ladies of the village, and got a hearty approval. We were surprised at the volume of sap these one hundred and seventy five trees produced. Each village family was given seven gallons of the syrup and we put a generous reserve stock in the Assembly storage closet. We also had a surplus of one hundred gallons. Medjet checked the price in the grocery stores and since it was all imported from eastern Canada it was expensive. We could package our maple syrup and sell it in the grocery stores. To our astonishment it was all gone off of the shelves in a week, the stores were asking for more and we had enough money to pay for all of the expenses we had incurred producing the syrup. Next year those profits would go into the building fund..

The tribe had its splendid stone building for the Assembly Hall, another for the Ladies Guild and now it was obvious there was a need for a large one for the Deerfoot artisans. The old steel shed that had first produced the totem poles was getting too small for the woodworkers, and the tribe was going to need another group of totem poles in the next few years.

Medjet announced at breakfast one day that she thought the baby would arrive at about the same time as we would celebrate the thirtieth anniversary of her father being elected chief. We had another cup of coffee as I absorbed the news delivered in that one package.

His life as chief had certainly had its ups and downs but the tribe had better do a bit of celebrating for his thirtieth anniversary.

I went over to see the artisan designer and explained about the anniversary. Could they design an imposing chair for the chief that would have two small totem poles as front legs and two larger ones for the back legs and have the ladies make leather cushions with Deerfoot symbols painted on them?

Five months later he showed me the chair. It was striking with the carefully painted miniature totem pole legs, front and back and the ladies had done a masterly job of painting and polishing the leather cushions. Jason had the chair carefully wrapped and hidden away until presentation day. I asked if Medjet could come over and see it, he paused for a moment and then said, "Yes, next Thursday afternoon."

They were ready for her when we came and she was appropriately impressed and told them so. They then brought out a rocking crib they had made for the baby, carved and painted with Deerfoot tribe symbols. It was the only time I ever saw Medjet without a word to say as she was so overcome by this gesture of affection and respect from these hard working men. They understood how much hard work she had put into the growth of the village and wanted to say a very personal Thank You.

Jason was the first to break the silence after Medjet had wiped the tears from her eyes and said, "By the way we must look forward to the making of another group of totem poles for the village.. While doing some of the undergrowth in the north block of land we have come across a group of magnificent red pine trees, tall and perfect for what we need. If the authorities could approve cutting about eight of them we could let them dry properly and begin carving in a couple of years."

Medjet nodded. Then Jason went on, "We have discovered something interesting in clearing the stumps in the north block of land. The glacier movement ages ago, dumped many large size rocks in that region. It makes it difficult to move our equipment but it has an offsetting benefit. Many of the trees have grown around or beside a rock and thus we get a strange shape of the bottom of the tree instead of the usual round one. The fellows have looked at some of the stumps and are quite excited about what we can get from them. We should have our village ladies look at them before we send them off to the shops in Victoria."

On the way home Medjet said, "You know, those men in the artisans shop have been making a sizable contribution to the village. Could we manage to build a large stone building in which they could be more comfortable and so better house their production lines?"

"There is a sizable check coming in from the provincial government, they earn a lot of money each year. We can probably arrange to do it next year. Let us get Alan thinking about a plan and get the quarry into production for the stone."

Chapter Nine

Medjet and I had gone to Vancouver for a few days leaving a happy grandmother to spoil the baby and take care of the place. We had gone to a lumber/hardware supply shop to find some drawer handles for the workshop. As we were browsing around, we saw a group of men gathered at one end of the shop. We went over to where the group was just in time to hear the auctioneer say, "This load on the third trailer is salvaged red oak planks. It has been immersed in salt water for a short time. Will someone give me an opening bid please."

There was a long moment of silence and then someone said, "Two thousand dollars."

"Four thousand dollars," I said.

"I have four thousand," said the auctioneer. "Any other bids?" Silence and then he said, "Going once going twice, going three times. Sold to the gentleman in the red jacket for four thousand dollars."

I paid the clerk and made arrangements to have the oak planks delivered to the village. Then as we walked away Medjet said, "Going to build a new doghouse for Gunner?"

"Jason will be more delighted than you can imagine."

When the woodworkers had moved into the new building we bought an exotic computer driven set of machines for carving and cutting the various pieces of wood needed.

A few weeks earlier Jason and I were walking to the new building and he said, "You know, these buildings are splendid but somehow the entrance doorways look unfinished. I have often wondered how we could enhance them a bit."

Medjet and I talked about this, invited Jason over for lunch and told him what I had done in the purchasing the oak planks. We invited him to make a first sample doorframe, carved with Deerfoot symbols. We would then put this impressive frame on the chief's house and then see how functional it was and how it added to the appearance of the building.

Jason and Medjet spent some time working out the interweaving of the Deerfoot symbols. Then Jason set the computer to do the carving on the planks. They were twelve inches by two inches. The outer frame was carved and given a number of coats of a good marine varnish. No color on these. When they put the frame together and looked at it, it was obvious that the existing door was not going to look right.

Jason said,"That is easy, we will make a new door out of the planks and with a new frame it will be just what is needed. Doors like this have existed in churches and other buildings in Europe for hundreds of years."

We invited the chief over to look at the assembled parts. He looked carefully at it and said, "It is a work of art, and you are to be congratulated. It will be a substantial addition to any building. Where is it going to go?"

"We thought it would look nice as the front door of your house."

"Ah, yes, you people never cease to amaze me. I will be proud and most grateful to have it. But do you have enough timber for the big buildings and the other houses? How did all this begin?" We told him the story.

It was lunchtime so we dispersed to give the woodworkers the afternoon to install the new door.

Unknown to Medjet and I, the chief and Jason got their heads together over lunch and Jason explained how I had come across the salvage sale and then how Medjet had helped with the design work. Then the chief said, "They never stop thinking about how to help the tribe, do they? Is there some way we could do something for them, or for their house?"

"I have been thinking about that for quite a while," Jason said. "I made a phone call to that lumber company to ask about these auctions. I was told they would have another next week. At present they have a small amount of that oak planking and the salvage timber from the teak deck of a thirty-year old ship that went down on the rocks in the Terra del Fuego channel. I would like to go to that auction."

"I'll get a cheque book from Medjet and we can go down to see if we can find something of value."

At the auction there was a trailer was full of various lengths of teak planks and other pieces taken from the sometime deck of the freighter. The oak planks were from the same group that we had.

Jason said, "Lets get them both if we can. The teak will be very valuable."

When the bidding opened and they came to the oak planking someone said, "There is not enough there for a major purchase, I'll bid fifty dollars."

The chief said, "Two hundred and fifty."

"No other bids, going once, going twice, going three times to the gentleman in the black jacket.

When they came to the trailer full of the teak pieces someone called out, "It is all small pieces not any use for veneer or building."

The auctioneer asked for bids and got a long silence in response. Then the chief raised his hand and offered, "Two hundred."

The auctioneer looked around then said, "Going once, going twice going three times for two hundred to the gentleman in the black jacket."

They made arrangements with a trucking company for delivery and then set out for home. Jason could not have been more pleased with the purchases.

"We will now have enough oak for every doorway in the village. We spoke about a Thank

You for Medjet and Jim since they have done so much for the village. Since we have enough teak to make a very elaborate front door entrance to their house, we can also make some pieces of furniture for them. I would like to make their front door entrance a really exciting work of art. If we have any of the oak left over I want to use it for making special frames for the many pictures that Medjet has painted for the big buildings. Also I would like to make two or three table lamps for each house. The lamp itself can be a miniature totem pole in full color. Think of how that would look in a living room. We should have floor lamps to match, but it will be tricky to get the design right.

Two weeks later Jason had the ladies of the Guild invite Medjet and I over to look at some designs they were working on. When they came in they saw an exquisite dining room table on the floor. The top was a herringbone pattern of teak pieces set in an oak frame. The ladies were making the leather cushions for the seat and back of the chairs that were to go with the set. The chief and Jason had come in while Medjet and I were exclaiming over the beauty of the table.

Then Jason looked at the chief, who nodded,

and Jason said, "We are pleased that you like the table and chairs. They are our gift to you as a small thank you for all you have done for the village." He went on to say, "There will be a set like this for every house in the village and we are making table lamps and floor lamps like these for every house." The ladies had brought out two table lamps and two floor lamps while he was speaking.

"These are yours."

"Medjet said, "This is the most work you have all done. They are beautiful and we are so grateful." She wiped away a few tears of happiness.

Jason said, "With computer driven carving and the design input every one is different. The hard work is done by the ladies painting the small totem poles. We are debating whether we should color the carved doorframes of the big buildings or should they just be left like the carved and varnished doorframes for the houses. In your case the teak is very hard and does not lend itself to paint absorption as other wood does. We have used teak wherever we could for your house. Only the table pedestals and lamps are oak. We have enough oak to make picture frames for all of your paintings but will need your advice on how these frames should be made and painted."

A week later they delivered all the items, assembled the heavy table in place, set up the lamps and then as a last gesture of affection they brought in an exotic new house for Gunner.

Two days later they invited Medjet and I to come to the Assembly Hall for a meeting of the Finance Committee. They had asked grandmother to come and babysit.

The meeting seemed to be dragging its feet and then we had an extended lunch and more meeting. At mid afternoon one of Jason's men looked in and nodded to Jason and left. The rest of the people seemed to understand the signal as the meeting was quickly adjourned and everyone went on their way.

When Medjet and I arrived home we understood what all the delaying tactics were about. Jason's men had remodeled the entrance to the house. The whole front wooden door and its frame had been removed and a teak door with brass hardware and carved patterns in wood had been installed. The same pattern extended over both side windows. It was the most beautiful design work I had ever seen, truly a masterpiece of the wood worker's art. Medjet stopped and then took another look in the bright afternoon light.

"I have never seen anything like it. It is simply stunning in the way it shows off the dark wood against the white stone background. How do we say Thank You to all these people?"

"In person when we meet them and again at the next Assembly."

But the next Assembly would be a different and a sad event. Medjet's father, after serving the tribe for more than thirty years came to the end of his life. The village was sad and silent. Medjet read the eulogy in which she emphasized the words which he had made so prominent in the lives of all of them; – Ask Not What The Tribe Can Do For You–Ask What You Can Do For The Tribe–words so vividly emblazoned on the front wall of the Artisans building, words each tribe member knew and understood.

The Assembly quickly set about an election of a new chief. The first name put in nomination was Medjet. She quickly nominated Jason. Jason withdrew his name and Medjet, by acclamation, became the first female chief of the Deerfoot tribe.
She was determined to change things as little as possible. Her mother would live out her days in the house and Medjet would hold council meetings there

as needed. She continued to live as she had, on Bear Paw Island.

The change that the oak doorways made in the appearance of the village was astonishing. The buildings themselves were impressive, the colorful totem poles and then the oak doors and frames as Jason carved them, created an appearance that was striking indeed.

The woodworkers had been busy with the interior tables, chairs and lamps with the distinctive carvings and the colorful leather cushions. The pride that every member of the tribe took in the place was always unspoken but clear to the eye of any observant person. Medjet made it clear in her report at Assembly, what the accomplishments of the various groups were. She also reported that she had received requests from a number of families, who had some Deerfoot ancestry, about the possibility of their moving to the village.

When baby George was eighteen months old his brother Jens arrived. As soon as Jens became mobile, they became inseparable and remained that way until they finished university and George got married. It was astonishing to watch them grow up together. We decided to get involved in a home schooling program rather than have them go back and forth to the city each day. There was never any sibling rivalry. What one learned, he transmitted to the other. By the time that Jens was sixteen they had written the senior high school examinations and won a scholarship. They were accepted at the University of British Columbia. Once started, they went through an arts degree on scholarships and then were admitted to law school.

In his second year George had discovered a student in the medical faculty whose maternal grandmother had been a Deerfoot. When she finished her internship George had completed his articling and they decided to get married.

They had some discussion about where they would live until she came up to the village for the first time. Then she did a careful inspection of the village and asked Medjet why there was no clinic.

Jens had decided to accept the Rhodes Scholarship offered and went to Oxford University.

Another year's building program began. Eight houses and a clinic building would be manageable within the available space allocation but we faced a problem. We had to make a careful selection of families who would fit into the village culture and be able to make a significant contribution to the growth of the village.

We found some temporary space in the Ladies Guild building and Alan and the new bride, Mazie, had some discussions as to what a clinic should have within its walls.

Medjet gave George the task of reviewing the applications for housing in the village and recommending which families should be chosen. This would, of course, require an in-depth investigation of all the circumstances of their lives. It would certainly take all the time available before the new buildings were ready for their occupants.

George found that he was a very busy fellow indeed. With his law degree and training in government structures he was an obvious candidate to eventually follow in Medjet's footsteps as chief of the tribe when she decided to be just a housewife, if that ever happened. She had used every moment that she could get away to work on her paintings in the studio. During the expansion period she had painted large forest and water scenes for the big buildings. Pictures that almost invariably got very favorable comments from visitors. A year before we had taken two of these into a gallery in Vancouver and, almost with tongue in cheek, put a twenty thousand sign on each. Imagine our surprise when they were gone in a week.

George made a comment about her spending time on trivia when her painting might produce more funds for the community. He took over as many of her duties as he could.

He was fascinated by what was coming out of the woodworking shop. We had one of Alan's people keeping an eye on the lumber auctions but it was unlikely we would ever find another bargain like we found in that shipment of oak planks. We would have to look at our options when that day arrived.

Chapter Ten

Medjet remembered that during the Minister's last visit he had said that he would like to see the building process when next we set a building program in motion. Medjet sent a message and we were told that he and a delegation would arrive four days after the House went into recess in April.

They looked carefully at the foundation for house number four and then went back to the second stage of the construction of the clinic.

I was off to one side watching all the action and the Minister came over to me and said, "I'm told that you are the one who started the whole process in motion here."

"Not really, I had heard of the process and found Alan Chan who had done his doctoral thesis on the history and current usage of the process in many other countries. He had been involved in building some of these structures on one of the islands. I had made enough money in a real estate venture in Vancouver to help fund the first building phase and then the thing took off."

"You don't live here?"

"No. I bought the island adjacent to the reserve on the waterfront side and we have a house there. Medjet is my wife."

"Then that is the house that I have heard about. An interesting geological formation I'm told."

We got into the truck and drove two minutes over to the house on Bear Paw Island. He paused and took a long look at the entrance that Jason had designed and fabricated, then said, "I've seen things like this in a few places in England but never this intricate. It is beautiful."

We went in, were welcomed by Gunner, and the Minister looked around in amazement at the polished stone of the walls, and just shook his head. He then went over to where he could look carefully at Medjets large painting on the wall, and after a careful look he said, "That should be in the National Gallery in Ottawa where a half a million people a year could see it. I know the chief curator there. Would you have a companion piece for him to buy if he came calling?"

"There are a half dozen of them in the village and he could have his choice. I'll have lunch ready in a few moments. Perhaps you would like a drink while I do the necessary?"

"I would indeed. I notice that you have a strict prohibition on alcohol on the reserve."

"Yes, anyone bringing alcohol on the reserve automatically goes before the council."

I poured a couple of honest drinks of scotch added a bit of ice water to each and we sat and chatted while Medjet made the lunch.

We sat at Jason's teakwood dining table and the whole ensemble drew a most favorable comment from our guest, the table itself and the magnificent decorated leather cushions of the chairs.

"This is the sort of stuff that should be in Rideau Hall or 24 Sussex Drive."

"This fish is wonderful," he said to Medjet..

She laughed and said, "At this time yesterday it was swimming out in the water in front of the house."

He finished his glass of wine, refused dessert and said, "The boys will think I have been kidnaped. I'd better get back. I'll see that you get another quick slice of the building fund money. Do you suppose we could get Alan down our way to talk to the House Committee about this method of building?".

The rest of the delegation had been well fed

by the ladies in the Assembly Hall, and had seen all they wanted, so the crew of their helicopter was soon on the stone park and then they were gone.

Medjet called a meeting of the council next day and explained how impressed the Minister had been with the table and the paintings.

"First and quickly, I'm going to send two of my best paintings to the Director of the National Gallery, with a covering letter explaining that they are a gift from the Minister. Then the Director can fuss over him with some formal presentation. Meanwhile, Jason, can you make something like a replica of this table to send to his house.? He has treated us very generously and we should be able to say, thank you. We will need more help before we are finished the current building program and I would like him to be receptive when the request hits his desk."

Two weeks later a truck arrived at the village. It was a large load of oak planks, sixteen feet in length two inch thick.

The driver said, "This stuff has been in a warehouse in southern Ontario for about twenty five years and I was told to deliver it here. Where do I unload it?"

Jason soon had the design drawings in hand and then they began the cutting. A few days later Medjet received a phone call from the Minister.

"My friend the Gallery Director is very excited about the possibility of a formal inauguration of a First Nations Room in the Gallery. I told him about the splendid Chief's chair which you have in the Assembly Hall. He wants to hold the reception with the Governor General and the Prime Minister there in August. Could you possibly give us two of those splendid chief's chairs, half a dozen of those leather cushions, two floor lamps and four table lamps all with the mini totem poles as their base?"

Jason and Medjet got their heads together to put more Canadiana and less Deerfoot in the designs and then they began the cutting. The painting was going to take the most time. So they worked long hours on all the items and, after a final inspection, they were sent on their way to the Gallery.

In mid July Medjet received an engraved invitation for the Deerfoot Chief and a guest to attend the inauguration ceremony for the First Nations display.

When we arrived at the Gallery we were scarcely in the door before the Minister came over to us with a warm welcome. He then introduced us to the Governor General and his wife, the Prime Minister and his wife and then to the Director.

A large crowd was in the room holding drinks and eating canapés.

When the Director rang a silver bell they all took their seats and the Minister took Medjet and I to the center of the front row. He then introduced the Governor General and the Prime Minister, and then thanked us all for coming. He introduced Medjet and I as the guests of honor as the main contributors to the display and Medjet as the painter of the pictures.

When the speeches were all done Medjet and I were standing off to one side looking at the crowd and we were surprised to have the Minister come over to us and say, "Could you spare a few minutes? His Excellency would like to talk to you ?"

We went over and were astonished to have the Governor General say, "My wife and I have wanted to have one of the reception rooms at Rideau Hall dedicated to the First Nations. We are very impressed with the display of imagination, design and color that the items shown this evening portray. Visiting heads of state and small delegations often come to Rideau Hall and a room fitted out with the kind of furniture and other items we have seen here this evening would be very Canadian and very impressive. Can you help us with items and the room design?"

Medjet said, "When would it be convenient for you to have us come over and look at the room you wish to use?"

" Would you be able to come over for coffee about ten tomorrow morning?"

"Of course. We are staying at the Chateau and can get a cab."

The Minister, who had been listening to the conversation said, "I'll have a car and driver ready for you when you want to go."

We were at Rideau Hall at ten and taken into a sunny reception room, warmly welcomed and given some coffee and Danish. Then it was on to the room they wanted decorated.

A large slightly arched doorway would be given a carved entrance, two paintings, two of the chiefs chairs, a number of other standard chairs with leather engraved cushions, floor lamps, table lamps and a ten foot long table with two pedestals, all noted in Medjet's sketchbook.

Then she said, "That doorway has been created

for a carved display but the person who can do it best must come and get the right perspective on the whole setting. It will take about a week to get him here but the end product will be worth the delay."

His Excellency smiled and waved Medjet to the telephone on a small table. She dialed and in a few minutes had Jason on the phone.

"Jason, we have been asked to help with a design and decoration problem in Rideau Hall. This is going to need your assessment and some measurements. How soon can you get down here to Ottawa?"

Jason wasted no time, and was in Ottawa the next day. Carefully measuring the doorway and the room interior he turned to Medjet and said, "What an opportunity to do some of the things I have been thinking of but had no place to try them. This archway needs a carved oak set of sliding doors, we need a ten foot long table, two chief's chairs and all the trimmings. If you and I can get the basic sketches done we can have all of this ready for installation in about two months or less. We must be cognizant of the other tribes so we don't get too many noses out of joint."

The GG came in and Medjet asked him if the

office of the Minister of Indian Affairs needed a bit of color.

"I've never been in it so do not know. But if you folks were to stay for lunch it would be time for the Minister to go to the House for question period. Then we could go to his office and you could have a look and see what might be done."

When we arrived the secretary was surprised to see the GG. She said the Minister was in the House. The GG asked her if we might look at the office and boardroom. Then he said, "Can you tell me when the Minister is going to be away for some time?"

"He will be in Geneva for the first week in September."

Jason had been taking layout sketches and measurements. He came out, nodded to Medjet so the GG said to the secretary, "I would greatly appreciate it if you did not mention our little visit to the Minister. We want to arrange a surprise for him."

Back to Rideau Hall, we said our goodbyes and the GG had his driver take us to the airport.

Jason and Medjet were in a special heaven that only artists know about as they made sketches of room layouts and items to be fabricated.

We asked the Ladies Guild and the Artisans

groups to meet in the Assembly Hall. Medjet explained what had happened and suggested it was an opportunity the like of which we would never see again.

She outlined in detail the layout at Rideau Hall and the Minister's suite. Two magnificent chief's chairs, one for the GG and a similar one for a visiting head of state, then the need for cushions of leather with the coats of arms on them for the other chairs. She suggested they make a dress set of a buckskin jacket for the GG and a skirt and blouse for his lady.

The Ladies Guild worked tirelessly on the painting and the cushions. Jason's woodworkers did the carving of the doorframes, the doors, picture frames and so on. The village was a very busy place.

In the last week of August two large trucks rolled up to Rideau Hall. Jason and his crew of woodworkers brought in the pieces and began to remove the existing structures and replacing them with the magnificent carved replacements.

Two of Medjet's large paintings in special carved frames, the herringbone table on its mini-totem pole pedestals, the two chief's chairs and all the other pieces were assembled.

Three days later they had cleaned out all the remnants of the earlier room and Medjet went to find the GG and his lady for their inspection.

Their delight at the new room could hardly be described. They examined all the carvings and the paintings and were very positive in their thanks. Then Medjet presented them with the Deerfoot buckskin jacket and the blouse and skirt for the lady. They called staff to bring in coffee and cakes and the GG put on his leather jacket.

He turned to Medjet and said, "I'm not sure how we will arrange payment for this but if you will give me an invoice I will see it through the payment process."

"There will be no invoice," Medjet said "this is a gift from the Deerfoot Tribe to the people of Canada in gratitude for all that Canada has given to us."

"Now Jason and his crew are going to have a few days to look around Ottawa before the Minister leaves for Geneva. Thank you for your hospitality, and the opportunity to serve the country."

Chapter Eleven

It didn't take long after the Minister's return to Ottawa for Medjet to get a phone call from him. He was very surprised on his return. Please give the Deerfoot Tribe his grateful thanks.

It was now the end of September, time for the semi-annual cull of the cattle and deer herds. This meant that the committee of the Ladies Guild would go each day to the meat packing plant and do the selection and wrapping of the meat for the tribe.
Each household received its share of beef and venison and the Assembly Hall kitchen was stocked for the Assembly dinners.

The October fish run had its committee out and they had a splendid catch of salmon for cleaning and distribution to each family.

I marveled at the legacy the old chief had left to the tribe. No one here ever asked what the tribe could and would do for its members, they only made sure they asked what they could do for the tribe.

An unwelcome, early snowfall arrived in November and the activities shifted to inside work for the Artisans and the Ladies Guild.

Spring was followed, as it had been for many years, by the University convocation. The tribe had a number of students attending. Five of them would be finishing this spring, so Medjet thought she and I and any parents who wanted to be there should go to the ceremonies.

The tribe graduates were visible in the assembly wearing their buckskin jackets. It was an impressive performance, two law scholarships to graduate school, two gold medals and one offer of a Rhodes' Scholarship.

For our small community it was an astonishing performance.

Later at the reception the Deerfoot people were in a group, conspicuous in our jackets, when the President of the University came over and said, "May I offer my personal congratulations on the achievements of you people."

Medjet said, "Thank you. The University has been good to us."

The President said, "There is one other thing I wanted to mention. I was recently a member of a group at a reception in Rideau Hall in Ottawa. The Governor General was very pleased to show the room that you decorated for the Hall. I wish we could afford such a room here at the university."

Medjet said, "Our design genius is right here. One of his children received a gold medal today. Could we see the room you would like to have decorated?"

"Thank you but we simply do not have the budget for such expenditure."

"The University has been very good to us over the years and there would be no cost to you for the design and installation. We would need only to see the room, do our measurements and then create all the necessary items and come and install them later as convenient for you."

"That certainly would be most gracious of you indeed."

The room was a large bland meeting room that had not had much attention in the past and Jason looked at his son and said, "What an unparalleled opportunity to show the Deerfoot capability. I can see a place for two of Medjet's large paintings, two large stained glass windows, oak carved frames for the doors and windows, two carved doors, three long tables, a chief's chair and other fittings. Jason looked at the drab overhead lighting fixtures and said, "Jens in all his genius could be turned loose on these lighting fixtures. Then turning to the President Jason said, "We can probably have it all ready for installation by mid-August and be out of the way in time for the student's arrival for the fall semester."

"We can be ready whenever you are." said the President.

Jason and his son finished their sketches and measurements and then we started off for the drive home.

It was a busy summer. The ladies had a plentiful supply of deer skins, the stained glass could be replenished as needed but Jason's oak planking was in short supply. We had our man in Vancouver keeping a watchful eye on the lumber auctions as they took place.

Early in August Jason told Medjet that they were ready to take all the pieces to Vancouver and assemble them as they re-did the room.

When they were finished, a week later, few people would have recognized it as the same room they started with. The President was invited to come and inspect the place. He brought his senior staff with him and the net effect was an almost speechless group. The carved doors were eye-catching but when they were opened and the visitors were treated to the magnificent color display of the paintings and windows it was reminiscent of some of the beauty one found in the old buildings in Europe. The visitors were hard pressed to believe that this decor had been done by a small group of Canada's First Nations. The pictorial presentation was all of indigenous Canada but the vehicles for showing that scenery had all been borrowed from another culture.

It took less than two weeks for the first request to arrive, with cheque attached, for one of Medjet's paintings. It was another nice contribution to the building fund. George suggested, that she resign all the duties of the chief's office and devote all her time to painting.

Jens and his stained glass committee received a delegation from a church in Prince Rupert asking for ten windows for their church.

Early in September the tribe was invited to send some representation to Ottawa to discuss the matter of how education on the reserves might be improved. The government was searching for ways to produce more educated professionals and tradesmen for the reserves and ways to keep more of their members out of jails and on the reserves.

When George, Medjet and I arrived at the Minister's office we were amused at the interest the various chiefs were showing in the room itself. They had all seen the brass plaque on the wall stating that the decor and items in the room had been designed and installed by the Deerfoot Tribe. One of the chiefs acidly said, "It would have helped, if all of us were invited to participate in the design and creation of the room."

Medjet looked at him for a moment and then said, "And what could you have contributed to the room?"

After a moment the Minister said, "May we open the discussion with a description of the situation on each of your reserves. Can we start with the first on the left and go around the table?"

The first chief reported that they had a continuing problem with attendance of the students in school so the classes became almost impossible for the teachers to manage. The next complained that the teachers who had been sent out seemed not to be able to maintain a reasonable discipline in their classes. The teachers usually gave up and left the school to go back to the city.

This litany of troubles went on with the chiefs

until they came to the Deerfoot representatives. Then Medjet stood up and said, "We do not have a school in the village. The children are taught in a classroom set up in the Assembly Hall. By the time the children are four years old they are reading and quickly getting to establish a wide vocabulary. The older students act as monitors and teachers of the younger ones. By the time they are sixteen years of age they all write the provincial senior high school examinations. They then make a decision as to whether they want to go to the community college in Prince Rupert or the university in Vancouver. Most of these students have earned scholarships so the cost of their education to the tribe is modest. We now have many skilled tradesmen and women and two lawyers going to graduate school on scholarships. Six students have been gold medalists, we have two Rhodes scholars, a medical doctor and support staff in a temporary clinic. In our next building program we will build a clinic to house the medical activities. In two years we will have our own dentist and support staff in the village. In the Ladies Guild there is the finest tailor training program in the province. In the artisan woodworking program we have the only woodworking and carving educational program in the province. Our home schooling program seems to be working very well. May I mention that the tribe has not had one penny of federal money for a school or related costs.

There was a long silence after she sat down. And then the next chief said, "There is not very much left to say after that recounting of accomplishments, except for us to learn how all this was done and try to do something like it in our reserves."

The Minister said, "It is now lunch time and I have invited a caterer to bring us some food. They should be here in a moment or two and we can continue our discussions over lunch."

The conference dragged on for the rest of the day and then wrapped up with no clear conclusions and no new directions for any one to follow.

On the way home Medjet said, "They seem unable to understand, that a new life on their reserves is only going to happen when they make it happen not when someone gives it to them. If they don't accommodate to modern day society and make the best of it and take the best of it, they will continue to flounder around not being part of a by-gone time or a part of modern society. They need to create their own new society–no one can give it to them."

When the next building program was finished we had thirty-six houses completed and a building fund that needed to be replenished. The cattle and deer herds were producing as much revenue as we could expect for the amount of grazing land we had available. All the land that had been forest at one time was now cleared of stumps and largely reforested.

Jason told the council that they had about a year's supply of tree stumps available and there was no replacement to be seen on the horizon.

Medjet contacted the Director of Crown Lands Authority and asked if the government had any plans for allowing timber cutting in the province. She was told that only very limited cutting of very large pine trees was allowed and these were small numbers indeed. However the Government of Alberta had opened up large tracts of timber stands in the western part of the province and might be glad to have the Deerfoot bid for land clearing and stump removal, if they were interested. They would pay the same price for removal as the British Columbia Government had paid.

Jason was asked to calculate whether the costs

of that removal could be absorbed and still keep the bowl production a source of income for the tribe.

In two years we would be able to increase our maple syrup production and make that a more lucrative source of funding. We were approaching some serious problems without quick solutions.

It was always nice to arrive home to a noisy welcome by Gunner. We decided to have a celebration dinner after the days of no accomplishment at the conference. Medjet had decided that she would turn over as much of the tribe's administration as possible to George and spend the time on her painting, as the list of cash customers was growing longer each week.

In a few days it will be Medjet's forty-fifth birthday. The tribe will meet in the Assembly Hall and we will all have a grand dinner to celebrate the occasion. As I look back down the years to that day in Victoria when we first met, I can hardly believe the things that have been accomplished in the village. Medjet's wise father once commented on how we might consider what we would be handing off to the next generation. I remember him saying in a reflective mood, one day, "Live each day, as if it were your last, one day you will get it right".

www.ingramcontent.com/pod-product-compliance
Lightning Source LLC
Chambersburg PA
CBHW070015110426
42741CB00034B/1882